FOUNDATIONS OF TEENAGE HAPPINESS

FINDING JOY AND PURPOSE IN THIS ADVENTURE CALLED LIFE

BY SCOTT CATT

Printed in the United States of America

First Printing, 2017

ISBN 978-1548462871

Birchwood Publishing

Cover and book formatting: Tanner Shelton Design

The Allazo Group
www.Allazogroup.com

ADVANCE PRAISE FOR FOUNDATIONS OF TEENAGE HAPPINESS

"Scott Catt hit the nail on the head with this one! He has a way of making you laugh, and reflect on your own life at the same time. Teenagers and adults alike can help themselves find and create their own happiness by following the principles in this book."

- Jessica Rex

Award Winning Junior High FACS Teacher

"The two things teens most want are in this book: more stories of what it looks like to live happily, and a great role model for this way of living. Scott's spirit comes through and gives teens the reassurance that he can be followed right down the road to happiness! As a champion of teens, truth, and teaching, I can recommend Scott's example and energy to anyone."

- Kari Avery

Owner, Avery Music Studio

"While Scotty's attention is focused to a younger teenage audience, I was struck with how his foundations for happiness really should apply to individuals of all ages. As I read his book, I was drawn into self-introspection on how I have lived my life and what changes I still need to make to fulfill my destiny in this life God has given us. His writing on happiness, if followed, would not only enrich the life of the teenage readers but also the lives of those around them. As Scotty states, "happiness is not simple action, it is a way of life". Kudos to Scotty for writing the book. I wholeheartedly endorse the book and will be passing it along to the youth (and adults) I encounter."

- John A. Freeze

Executive, Community Ambassador and Mentor to Youth

"Scott's "Foundations of Teenage Happiness" perfectly combines theory and application, through personal experiences and stories every teenager can relate to! It is engaging and applicable to any teen and will absolutely teach them the fundamental values to build a happier life. More than that it is applicable to any one, young or old, and will set them on the course to a happier and more purpose driven existence!"

- Mitchell A. Baker

MBA, High School State Championship Wrestler, Executive, and Former Teenager

"In his book Scott Catt lays out a systematic way in which teens can begin to make positive changes in their lives. His empathy is evident as he offers a wonderful combination of authentic experiences as well as quotes and quips from enlightened people throughout history. His easy, accepting language enables people to realize, that there is a way to live a happier life. The book is uplifting and comforting. It's interactive reflections make it a perfect tool in any middle or high school classroom. It is a must read for all teens."

- Beth Cirzan

Award winning High School English teacher

"This Book is just what the youth of this generation need! It is both relatable and applicable in so many ways. I will be applying various principles into my own life as a high school teacher and hopefully into the lives of many students I interact with. It is organized, easy to understand, and makes you feel like the author is writing specifically to you. I would recommend this book to any of my students!"

- Jessie Howard

Teacher, Coach and Stand Out College Athlete

"Too often we do not offer a holistic and thorough approach towards personal happiness for audiences younger than 25. We assume those books and those discussions are only respected by a "more experienced" and older crowd. Scotty does not make this assumption. He does not look at teenagers as just kids hanging out, instead they are people growing and evolving who deserve to know how to love themselves better NOW-- not in their 30s but now. This book teaches every lesson I am still in the process of learning however many years later. My only sadness about this book is that it was not in my hands as a teenager."

- Nicolle Okoren

Syndicated Author, Music Critic and YouTube Personality

DEDICATION

To Mom and Grandma and Grandpa x 2, Thank you for sacrificing so much to always put Scotty, Travis and Kord's happiness first.

TABLE OF CONTENTS

SECTION 1
INTRODUCTION

GENUINE BEGINNINGS BEGIN WITHIN US, EVEN WHEN THEY ARE BROUGHT TO OUR ATTENTION BY EXTERNAL OPPORTUNITIES.

- SIR WILLIAM THROSBY BRIDGES
SENIOR AUSTRALIAN ARMY OFFICER,
ORDER OF ST. MICHAEL AND ST. GEORGE

PREFACE

While in high school I found myself drawn to the Sports Medicine program and worked after school in the Athletic Training Room all four years. I fell in love with the profession early on and had the unique opportunity to know this is what I wanted to do with the rest of my life. For me, it was that simple, I would attend college to become an athletic trainer. Over the years I have worked with hundreds (probably thousands) of teenaged athletes. As an athletic trainer I am in charge of the health and medical care of every athlete on campus and in an unusual position in which I was there for the teenagers simply to help them, I did not need or expect anything from them in return. What I mean is that I was not their teacher who wanted them to do classwork, I was not their coach who wanted them to perform well on the field and court, I was not their parent wanting them to do chores, homework, etc., I was not their boss wanting them to work, you get the idea. I was truly there just for them, to support them, to help them, to try to make them better. In this position, I had many athletes open up to me and be more honest with me than the majority of others around them. What I found was that teenagers should enjoy being young and dumb (we all made dumb mistakes in our teenage years that now make for great stories to reminisce), but they're actually so stressed out and unhappy.

Three years ago, I began teaching high school sports medicine as well as continuing to be an athletic trainer after school. I have known for a long time that helping students makes me happy and teaching allows me to connect and help many more students. Teenagers are extremely stressed out. I knew that something had to change to make these teenagers happier and (at the expense of being cliche) I had to be the change. I had no training in how to be an educator and have had to learn on the fly. Foundations of Happiness puts into words the exact way I've tried to teach my students how to be happy and how to excel at life. This book epitomizes the teacher I strive everyday to become, and I am so glad to have found this resource. This book is a perfect hybrid of serious content, wit, and funny anecdotes. I intend to integrate this book into my curriculum as weekly bellwork. Scott explains the physical effects of unhappiness vs. happiness on our health and focuses on Mind, Body, and Heart (non-anatomical). Scott discusses the difference between short-term and long-term hapiness. He states the ways that our own mind can steal our happiness and ways to combat negative self-thoughts. This is something that I constantly teach and will definitely utilize the portion on how to change your internal monologue. I once heard and now use the phrases "positive mental attitude" and "is that helpful or hurtful" and Scott's examples will provide me more ways to teach how to change negative self-thoughts. Most importantly, Scott discusses service and giving to others. I was raised in a loving household that put much emphasis on this, and I agree with Scott's assessment that helping others selflessly brings true happiness. The book outlines specific examples of initial steps that teenagers can use to work towards service in their life. Scott and I went to high school together. He was always one of the popular guys, was always in a good mood, and was always helping others. The stereotypical "popular kids" that we think of and see in movies tend to be stuck-up, mean, and selfish, basically the movie "Mean Girls." Scott silently performed small acts of kindness and service during school that shifted what was meant by "popular" at our school. You will read examples throughout the book that show the way he lived these words as a teenager.

Scott has dedicated his life to helping others, especially teenagers, to improve themselves and to be happy. In an age in which social media, unrealistically high expectations, and accusations of laziness rules the teenage lifestyle, it is so refreshing to have an author who empathizes with them and sincerely wants to help these young adults be happy. Scott's voice throughout the book is so clear, candid, and moving. Written so simply, and yet so profound, this book is an easy read and applicable to all ages, not just teenagers. Scott truly understands the mindset of teenagers and pushes for them to attain happiness while providing them building blocks of how to work towards that goal.

I hope you enjoy this book and find it's usefulness in your everyday life, like I have.

Best Wishes,

-Lauren Krasner

Sports Medicine Teacher, Head Athletic Trainer, Health Occupations Students of America Advisor, Individual Striving for Daily and Lifelong Happiness

FORWARD

For parts of my teenage years, happiness consisted of some combination of a PlayStation, pizza, and procrastination. This lasted for about 6 or 7 hours, until I would notice my brain starting to leak out of my ears. When I finally crawled out of the basement, I'd search for something interesting to do, usually getting dragged by a parent/sibling/friend into doing some sort of seemingly-boring activity. I found myself doing Debate Team and triathlons, making new friends with people I'd never met before, and coaching a kids' swim team.

(I'll jump in real fast to say ¡DON'T WORRY! I'm not leading into a really cheesy story with a boring moral about how "I started to realize that I didn't need a pizza or a PlayStation!". Let's be real: if you're a teenager that ISN'T eating pizza by the pound and wasting time having fun, you're doing something wrong. Ok, glad we got that figured out, I'll get back to my story)

All of these activities SOUND a lot less fun than pizza and PlayStation (or whatever your time-wasting activity of choice is; I don't discriminate), and they kind of are. It isn't always really that FUN to train for a triathlon, or to coach kids whose swimming stroke was less "butterfly" and more "drowning kitten."

However, when I took some pizza and PlayStation time and replaced it with these worthwhile activities, I found myself becoming noticeably more HAPPY! I wasn't always having fun, but my experiences felt meaningful: I made friends doing Debate Team and meeting new kids at school, felt good about my body and fitness doing triathlons, and loved spending time with the kooky kids on that swim team. I learned new skills and grew out of my comfort zone, and I look back on those memories very fondly.

(Last time I'll interrupt: PLEASE don't stop eating pizza or procrastinating term papers, PLEASE! There's too many term papers in adulthood, you should procrastinate them while you're 13. Ok, I hope I got that sorted out.).

Even as a teenager, there's a lot of good you can do in the world for a lot of people. People out there need you and your unique talents, no matter who you are (sorry, I'm getting sappy, I know. I promised myself I wouldn't do this!). Reach out to others and make new friends, even if you're shy. Share your lunch money even if it means a 6-inch at Subway instead of a footlong. Try a new sport, join a new club: make new friends, and then go play video games with them.

Scotty Catt was my roommate when I was 17, and he did a dang good job of both eating pizza with me AND showing me how to be a happier person. Reader, this book is like having Scotty Catt as a roommate. He'll teach you concrete steps you can take to be happier, and you'll be too busy laughing to wonder whether a book about "the principles of happiness" is boring or not.

The only issue with the book is that there's no pizza. We'll get that in the 2nd Edition.

-Peter Fuller
Business person, Person person, former teenager (though I forever will act as mature as a 13-year-old), current adult (sort-of).

INTRODUCTION

Of all the things we strive for in life, happiness is at the top of the list! Life is an adventure and sometimes people don't end up where they thought they would when the adventure started. Most people spend their entire life looking for those things that really make them happy. Some people find them, others waste an entire life and never find true happiness. The key to their failure is they are consistently looking in the wrong places. It's been that way since the beginning of time. This transcendent journey may be the most important quest ever undertaken. Poets, philosophers, religious leaders, educators and psychologists alike have dedicated their lives to the pursuit of that universal question: What REALLY

FOUNDATIONS OF TEENAGE HAPPINESS

makes us happy?

Here's the thing, we are in luck! We know more about happiness and what really makes people happy than ever before! You are one of those people, in case you were wondering. Some of what we know is rooted in ancient philosophy applied to our modern context, other ideas come from this new emerging science. It fascinates me that we, as the human race, have put a man on the moon but only just now are turning our attention to putting happiness into our lives. Yet, when it comes down to it, that's what this book is all about; true, authentic happiness. More important than exploring the moon or the depths of the ocean, it is essential that you understand the universe inside of YOU. This is the path to finding peace and fulfillment.

But hear me out, this book is written for you, my teenage friends! All of us who have been teenagers know just how tough it can be. Some of the most successful people in the world battled the same battles you may be going through right now. Famed actress Aimee Teegarden stated, "No matter where you are or

12

where you grow up, you always go through the same awkward moments of being a teenager and growing up and trying to figure out who you are." JK Rowling, who changed the lives of countless teenagers through her epic story of Harry Potter, himself a teenage wizard, reflected on her own teenage years. "In fact, you couldn't give me anything to make me go back to being a teenager. Never. No, I hated it."

If being a teenager is rough for you, you are in good company. If you love it, go make someone's life a little easier. Either way, if you are looking to avoid all trials and live a life of complete bliss and fantasy, you are probably in for a rude surprise. However, as hard as being a teenager can be, it doesn't need to be a miserable experience. In fact, it can be a wonderful, joyful experience, filled with meaning and purpose. It all just depends on what you want and what you are willing to do to get there.

This book will help you! You can be happy! You deserve to be happy! And this book will teach you how to be happy, not just today, but for the rest of your life! Don't believe me? I dare you to try what's being taught, diligently, for a month. The proof will be there, and probably in a much shorter time than those four short weeks.

But how do we even begin to approach happiness? A sucker for analogies, I came up with one for you. I'm proud of it (It took me a whole five minutes), so take it easy on me! It works like this… Imagine you are building a house. Where do you start? You don't need to have any knowledge of construction to know you don't start with the roof! Logic also tells you that you don't start with the windows, the upstairs shower or the ceiling fans. To build a sturdy house you have to start with the foundation. Without the foundation to hold the rest of the house up, nothing else matters! Once the foundation is in place, you can build the house however you'd like, complete with windows, a Jacuzzi, golfing tees off your balcony, and a soda dispenser in the living room.

That's how happiness works (not the soda dispenser part). There are foundational principles that, if practiced, WILL make you happy. These foundations of happiness are principles on which you CAN and SHOULD build your life. I am here to teach you these principles. Together we will explore the Foundations of Teenage Happiness as it applies to you. Your world. Your adventure. Your life.

As you proceed through this book, there are several things I want you to do:

First, make this book personal to you. Take notes on your phone or tablet. If you need to, keep a piece of paper and pen next to you as you read, and write down the thoughts and ideas that come to your mind. If you are reading the print version of this book, write all over the margins, the back pages, over my picture, or wherever you want. I am certain that there will be more ideas that come to your mind that apply to YOUR happiness than there are words in this book. But here's the catch, if you don't write those thoughts down, they can never grow to become something of substance. Read passages over as you need to, skip around, and find what works for you!

Second, I want you to treat this book as something interactive! Use the principles being taught. Try new things. Put what is being presented to practice and keep track of how it's working! And finally, share what you learn. This book and these foundational principles will be a powerful tool in your life. As you will discover later, one of the greatest ways to find joy in your journey is to serve others. Sharing something that is changing your life in order to lift another is noble and exhilarating! Much like the light and power of a roaring fire, the illuminating flames only grow stronger when spread. If they are left to themselves, just like the tiny glow of a match, the flame will eventually go out only to leave you with darkness.

So now that we understand each other, here is how this book is going to go. We will be exploring the four main areas of YOUR life where it is absolutely essential to create these positive foundations of happiness. We'll start with foundations of the mind, exploring how we can create key practices that will affect our mental health and, you guessed it, our happiness. Second, we'll explore foundations of the body, how our physical health is directly linked to our long term…. Again you guessed it, happiness. Third, we'll discuss foundations of the heart, the essence of giving and connecting with others and how that will exponentially grow your... care to guess? Happiness. Finally, we would be missing something crucial if we didn't delve into the foundations of the soul and how the essence of who you are and what you stand for creates a lifetime of LASTING happiness. The key there is lasting, meaning enduring, able to withstand the trials of life, sticking power, i.e.... A long time!

- Scotty Catt

Author, of this Book, President of the Allazo Group, Friend of Youth, Former Teenager

WHY HAPPINESS MATTERS

"I am the Captain of my fate, I am the master of my soul."
-William Ernest Henley, English Poet and Author of "Invictus"

So now that you know WHAT we're going to study together, it's important that we spend some time talking about WHY we need to understand the foundations of happiness. Without the WHY behind what you're studying, the WHAT seems pretty useless, right? Like in math class when someone always asks, and for some reason it's always in a high pitched tone, "When will we use this in the real world?" And then your teacher tells you something like 150 scenarios where you will use it in the real world. Then the math becomes real. All of a sudden people start taking notes like your school was giving away free puppies and scholarships to the best note takers at the end of class. Same thing here. Just without the puppies or scholarships!

So let's get real for a second. There are some pretty terrible consequences that are associated with stress, something most teenagers know a thing or two about! But these same teenagers don't realize what stress has done to them as they grow into adults, with no chance to go back to those teenage years and change their destiny. Here are a few examples of the negative effects of stress, do any of them ring true?

- **It Drives Away Happiness** Obvious, but sometimes we forget what real happiness feels like until we remove the major stresses from our life. It's like someone who lives in pain for so long that forgets what it's like to feel normal and just end up accepting the pain as a reality. Lift that pain with a surgery or medication and their whole world changes.

- **Being Constantly Tired** We run ourselves ragged trying to keep up with everything we think we need to do but then when we do find time for sleep, we don't sleep well.

We start falling asleep in class, on the bus, in the middle of conversations. We feel like no matter what we do, we're never going to get over the feeling of constant, deflating, fatigue. Multiply that by years! it's not a happy life.

- **Frequent Sickness** Super stressed out people get sick A WHOLE LOT more than non-stressed out people. It's just a fact. If you tell me you are constantly sick, I am going to ask if you are constantly stressed. After which, I am going to tell you to go see a doctor. Why? Because I'm not one.

- **Low Self Esteem** You deserve to have high self-esteem! I am convinced that everyone in this world has something amazing to offer, but if you are constantly stressed, your mind will always be focused on that stress and never focused on the amazing person you are and the profound difference you can make on the world.

- **Anxiety** The majority of mental health issues come back to anxiety. Sadly, much of that anxiety links back to stress. Whether that is warranted or unwarranted it doesn't matter, it affects you the same. High levels of anxiety lead to even more serious problems down the road, roads we don't even want to cross, much less travel down.

- **Higher Chance of Addiction** Addiction has ruined millions of lives and destroyed countless families and friendships. Let that sink in. Massive devastation. When someone self medicates for stress with drugs or alcohol, it leads to these crippling addictions. If stress can lead to something so horrible, then let's attack it together and replace it with something glorious.

And now that you are feeling all stressed about feeling stressed, hear this, or read it, or whatever. There is extraordinarily good news! If we infuse our lives with happiness, there are some benefits that will change everything! First of all you get to lower the risk of all of these soul sucking party crashers listed above and, well, you get to be happy! Authentically happy. On top of that, here are a few other things worth noting:

- **Happiness Helps You to Focus!** Studies show that happy people can focus longer and with more precision when they are filled with happiness. This kind of focus can be seen in relationships, in school, and in everyday tasks.

- **Happiness Will Keep You Healthy!** Happy people are proven to be healthier people. They live longer. They enjoy more energy. They are less sick and more enthusiastic about life. Common cold? Less likely to get it. Migraines? Lower chance of it happening. Chronic back pain? Forget about it.

- **Happiness Will Combat Stress and Lengthen Your Life!** Stress will always be present, that's a part of life. But happiness is the precise antidote for stress. Stress is shown to shorten people's lifespan. When you are consistently happy, you are literally adding years to your life. Think of all the things you want to do in this life! You need time to make it happen. Happiness gives you the opportunity you need.

- **Happiness Helps Strengthen Your Friendships and Bonds With Family!** Relationships are never stagnant. They are either moving forward or moving backwards. Families and relationships can be ruined by stress built up over years of neglect. On the flip side, family relationships and friendships can continuously grow and enrich our lives as we remove unnecessary stress and, instead, add optimal happiness and love.

- **Happiness Leads You to a MUCH Higher Chance of Success in Life!** Michael Jordan always said he was "a firm believer in luck", because the harder he worked, the luckier he got. I think there was another component to his "luck," his Airness genuinely loved playing basketball. It made him happy and filled his life with excitement. When we're doing what makes us happy in life, we work harder because we want to. When we do what we hate, it's almost impossible to be happy. And, let's be honest, we never work hard enough to find success when we are consistently doing something we hate.

- **Happiness Helps You Find Purpose and Love!** I want to be happy. I want to have purpose. I want to love and be loved. How about you? I literally cannot think of a more fulfilling life than that. Purpose brings excitement to our lives every day and helps us connect with a higher calling. Something so much bigger than ourselves. True love is far different than infatuation, it lasts and endures. In the words of the French novelist, "There is only one happiness in this life, to love and be loved."

And those just name a few of the incredible benefits associated with happy people! So, if you have to pick one or the other, to pick between constant stress and enduring happiness (which, by the way, you kind of do) which would you choose? A tired, stressed out, life full of sickness? Or a life full of passion, fun, health and friendship? Yeah, me too. I feel like we're on the same page. So let's get into the foundations. It's time to build your life.

SELF-REFLECTION: _____

_____

_____

_____

_____

_____

_____

_____

_____

_____

_____

_____

_____

_____

_____

_____

_____

_____

_____

_____

_____

_____

_____

_____

_____

SECTION 2
THE FOUNDATIONS

WHATEVER YOU DO, OR DREAM YOU CAN,
BEGIN IT. BOLDNESS HAS GENIUS AND
POWER AND MAGIC IN IT.

- JOHANN WOLFGANG VON GOETHE
FAMED GERMAN WRITER AND STATESMAN

FOUNDATIONS OF THE MIND

"I am still determined to be cheerful and happy, in whatever situation I may be; for I have also learned from experience that the greater part of our happiness or misery depends upon our dispositions, and not upon our circumstances."
- Martha Washington   America's Very First, First Lady

The mind, in so many ways, is the gateway to happiness. Buddha was credited with saying it first, but countless incredible people have echoed the concept since.

"To enjoy good health, to bring true happiness to one's family, to bring peace to all, one must first discipline and control one's own mind. If a man can control his mind he can find the way to Enlightenment, and all wisdom and virtue will naturally come to him."

Does that mean that you need to think happy thoughts and all your problems will go away? No! There's more to it. Of course your thoughts are tied to your actions and decisions, and they are crucial in creating the outcome you desire. So think positive thoughts! Then there is the question that always comes up. Does that mean that mental illness should be ignored as something that is just created by negative thinking? Absolutely not! Let me make that clear, though these foundations are key to creating lasting happiness, mental illness is real and should be treated by a medical professional. If you are struggling with a mental illness, it is nothing to be ashamed of. We wouldn't tell someone with a broken leg to walk it off, and it would be equally inappropriate to tell someone with a legitimate mental illness to cowboy up and get over it. So if that's your battle in life right now, keep fighting the good fight, get the help you need, and if some of these foundational principles help you, by all means counsel with your healthcare professional and use them!

With that said, let's explore where happiness and just about everything else starts, the most relevant last frontier, our own minds.

IT STARTS WITH THE MIND

You think all the time (I hope!), but how often do

you think about what you're thinking about? Was that too confusing? Read it again, because I stand by the principle! The mind is perhaps the most powerful tool in your life for creating peace and prosperity on the one hand or destruction and distress on the other. We need to pay attention to our mind! For those having a hard time following, Your Mind on Autopilot= Bad, Your Mind on Manual Control= Good.

A mind is something that everyone has but very few people even attempt to understand! Think about it! Everything you do in your life starts in your mind. Something starts as a thought, then it becomes multiple thoughts, then a decision, and ultimately an action! I like pizza; I want a pizza; I am going to order a pizza; I ordered the pizza; and now, I am eating the pizza. Snap. It's that simple. So if we wanted to change our actions, where would we start? Of course it comes back to our thoughts! I want a pizza... but wait, pizza isn't great for me, and I want to spend the little cash I have on a new air freshener for my car-because... dates. No ordering the pizza, no eating the pizza, higher chance of your next date going well.

Destiny altered. You're welcome.

So here's a practice to live by: Check your thoughts and ask yourself where they are going to lead you. In the case of the pizza, if thinking through it isn't enough, move your phone so you can't order your pizza, turn off your computer for the same reason, and go to the fridge and eat something else to change your mindset. This practice works in almost every scenario of our life. Our thoughts are going to lead us somewhere; we might as well do everything in our power to make sure it's where we want to go.

OUR MINDS ARE LIKE A GARDEN

James Allen, a brilliant philosopher on the power of the mind who lived over a century ago, provided powerful insights on your happiness and its connection with your thoughts. He made this point, comparing our minds to a garden in his book, *As a Man Thinketh* (A book everyone should read, by the way), "A man's mind may be likened to a garden, which may be intelligently cultivated or allowed to run wild; but whether cultivated or neglected, it must, and will, bring forth. If no useful seeds are put into it, then an abundance of useless weed seeds will fall therein, and will continue to produce their kind."

Essentially, what Allen is saying is that if we don't choose what goes into our mind, the world and our surroundings will choose for us! And in a world filled with negativity, pessimism, and filth, we are asking for trouble when we let that kind of influence run free in our mind! At the same time, if we choose to garden our thoughts, removing those negative thoughts and replacing them with positive, empowering and uplifting ideas, we will eventually have a mind that is capable of sustaining happiness! Happiness, positivity, great relationships, optimism, health… It's a total win across the board.

Another practice to live by: Garden your thoughts. Most negative self-talk, meaning the things we say to ourselves in our own mind, is a lie, plain and simple. Pay attention to what you are thinking. When something enters your mind that isn't positive or helpful, remove it by repeating something out loud that is true and uplifting. Do this as many times as you have to until it sticks! I'm serious, even if it takes a couple of hours or a couple of days, do whatever you can to get that negative self-talk as far away from your mind as humanly possible.

EXPECT THE NATURAL RESULTS OF YOUR ACTIONS

I have a dear friend who taught me a powerful principle. We were talking to an associate who was going through a hard time. Here's the catch, every single one of her problems had to do with one or another horrible decision she had made over the space of many years. She wasn't ignorant to that fact either; she knew full well what the consequences would be for her actions and she was experiencing those consequences in full effect. I expected my friend to offer some sort of comfort like, "It's going to be ok! You're an amazing person! It's not your fault!", you know, the standard, easy way out of an awkward situation, kind of talk. But instead he faced the whole thing head on and told her something he had learned as a youth and something we all would do well to remember. He said, simply but confidentially, "You need to remember, bad decisions make you sad. Good decisions make you happy."

Our friend actually took that really well; in fact, it became a theme she would live by. But as I thought about those simple truths my friend was taught in childhood, I realized how profound they really are! How ridiculous are we to think that somehow making bad decisions, that we know are destructive, counterproductive, and always bring us heartache, will one day magically make us happy? It makes no sense! It's ridiculous! Yet we all do it in one way or another. It was Albert Einstein who said that the definition of insanity is doing the same thing over and over the same way and expecting different results. So by Professor Einstein's definition, you have all been guilty of insanity at one time or another.

At the same time, we can feel assured that if we make good choices, they will eventually lead to happiness, prosperity, and authentic love. It may not happen immediately; we may have down days, but we will ultimately be happy! Things may not go our way all the time, but they are more likely to. Moreover, we are given one of the greatest gifts in this life, peace of mind, knowing we are doing the right thing for the right reasons. Just remember, it is impossible to have chronic negative thoughts and simultaneously have the constantly happy life you deserve.

SELF-REFLECTION: _____

_____

_____

_____

_____

_____

_____

_____

_____

_____

_____

_____

_____

_____

_____

_____

_____

_____

_____

_____

_____

FOUNDATIONS OF TEENAGE HAPPINESS

_____

_____

_____

_____

_____

_____

_____

_____

_____

_____

_____

_____

_____

_____

_____

_____

_____

_____

_____

_____

_____

_____

42

FOUNDATIONS OF THE BODY

"Optimism is a happiness magnet. If you stay positive, good things and good people will be drawn to you."
- Mary Lou Retton   Olympic Gold Medal Winning Gymnast

Our body and mind are connected. They are intertwined and inseparable. In so many ways, to neglect the one is to neglect the other. When our bodies are healthy, our minds have a much better chance of being healthy. When the two are working in unison, happiness abounds.

So what is happiness really and how does it relate to the body? Happiness can only really be defined by you. If we were to try and define it, a possible definition could be "a state of well-being or contentment." Or possibly we could go with an "ongoing state of satisfaction and joy." Perhaps we could even try some synonyms; cheerfulness, peace, well-being, or joy. I might even throw the word peace in there. But in short, the test to really figure out what happiness means to you is to determine if what you are experiencing brings joy, cheerfulness, or peace for a long, sustained period of time.

So you may be asking, why are we talking about this now? Because when it comes to the body, it is too easy to confuse temporary satisfaction with actual, authentic happiness. The only way to avoid the devastating effects of following the path of fleeting satisfaction is to know the difference between those good feelings that are momentary and those joyous feelings that are lasting. To understand the difference is true happiness, to confuse the difference is misery.

THE POWER OF POSITIVITY

Positive people are healthier people. I think we have all seen that in action. But, I am going to go ahead and quote the experts, bringing in the real cowboys so to speak. This is an article from the Mayo Clinic Staff. You can find it in its entirety on their website. Get ready to be amazed. The article starts with this preface:

Positive thinking: Stop negative self-talk to reduce stress

Positive thinking helps with stress management and can even improve your health. Practice overcoming negative self-talk with the examples provided. On the next few pages you will find an excerpt from an article written by the staff at the world renowned Mayo Clinic.

By Mayo Clinic Staff

Is your glass half-empty or half-full? How you answer this age-old question about positive thinking may reflect your outlook on life, your attitude toward yourself, and whether you're optimistic or pessimistic — and it may even affect your health.

Indeed, some studies show that personality traits such as optimism and pessimism can affect many areas of your health and well-being. The positive thinking that usually comes with optimism is a key part of effective stress management. And effective stress management is associated with many health benefits. If you tend to be pessimistic, don't despair — you can learn positive thinking skills.

Understanding positive thinking and self-talk

Positive thinking doesn't mean that you keep your head in the sand and ignore life's less pleasant situations. Positive thinking just means that you approach unpleasantness in a more positive and productive way. You think the best is going to happen, not the worst.

Positive thinking often starts with self-talk. Self-talk is the endless stream of unspoken thoughts that run through your head. These automatic thoughts can be positive or negative. Some of your self-talk comes from logic and reason. Other self-talk may arise from misconceptions that you create because of lack of information.

If the thoughts that run through your head are mostly negative, your outlook on life is more likely pessimistic. If your thoughts are mostly positive, you're likely an optimist — someone who practices positive thinking.

The health benefits of positive thinking

Researchers continue to explore the effects of positive thinking and optimism on health. Health benefits that positive thinking may provide include:

- Increased life span
- Lower rates of depression
- Lower levels of distress
- Greater resistance to the common cold
- Better psychological and physical well-being

- Better cardiovascular health and reduced risk of death from cardiovascular disease
- Better coping skills during hardships and times of stress

It's unclear why people who engage in positive thinking experience these health benefits. One theory is that having a positive outlook enables you to cope better with stressful situations, which reduces the harmful health effects of stress on your body.

Focusing on positive thinking

You can learn to turn negative thinking into positive thinking. The process is simple, but it does take time and practice — you're creating a new habit, after all. Here are some ways to think and behave in a more positive and optimistic way:

- **Identify areas to change.** If you want to become more optimistic and engage in more positive thinking, first identify areas of your life that you usually think negatively about, whether it's work, your daily commute or a relationship. You can start small by focusing on one area to approach in a more positive way.

- **Check yourself.** Periodically during the day, stop and evaluate what you're thinking. If you find that your thoughts are mainly negative, try to find a way to put a positive spin on them.

- **Be open to humor.** Give yourself permission to smile or laugh, especially during difficult times. Seek humor in everyday happenings. When you can laugh at life, you feel less stressed.

- **Follow a healthy lifestyle.** Aim to exercise for about 30 minutes on most days of the week. You can also break it up into 10-minute chunks of time during the day. Exercise can positively affect mood and reduce stress. Follow a healthy diet to fuel your mind and body. And learn techniques to manage stress.

- **Surround yourself with positive people.** Make sure those in your life are positive, supportive people you can depend on to give helpful advice and feedback. Negative people may increase your stress level and make you doubt your ability to manage stress in healthy ways.

- **Practice positive self-talk.** Start by following one simple rule: Don't say anything to yourself that you wouldn't say to anyone else. Be gentle and encouraging with yourself. If a negative thought enters your mind, evaluate it rationally and respond with affirmations of what is good about you. Think about things you're thankful for in your life.

Here are some examples of negative self-talk and how you can apply a positive thinking twist to them:

Putting positive thinking into practice

Negative self-talk	Positive thinking
I've never done it before.	It's an opportunity to learn something new.
It's too complicated.	I'll tackle it from a different angle.
I don't have the resources.	Necessity is the mother of invention.
I'm too lazy to get this done.	I wasn't able to fit it into my schedule, but I can re-examine some priorities.
There's no way it will work.	I can try to make it work.
It's too radical a change.	Let's take a chance.
No one bothers to communicate with me.	I'll see if I can open the channels of communication.
I'm not going to get any better at this.	I'll give it another try.

Practicing positive thinking every day

If you tend to have a negative outlook, don't expect to become an optimist overnight. But with practice, eventually your self-talk will contain less self-criticism and more self-acceptance. You may also become less critical of the world around you.

When your state of mind is generally optimistic, you're better able to handle everyday stress in a more constructive way. That ability may contribute to the widely observed health benefits of positive thinking.

ABSOLUTE MIC DROP BY THE MAYO CLINIC STAFF! But then I pick it back up because I actually have more to say…

WE ARE WHAT WE PUT INTO OUR BODY

When it comes to taking care of your physical self, Jim Rohn may have said it best. "Take care of your body, it's the only place you have to live." And that's true! There is no motel down the road where you can crash. You have one body, one opportunity to take care of it. Think about what you put into your body every day. What does it say about you?

When we make it a habit to put healthy things into our body, we are more likely to experience joy, energy, and feelings of happiness. As well as, shocker, health. When we put junk into our body, we feel like junk; we have less energy; we get sick more often and are more likely to experience bouts of depression. The contrast really couldn't be any clearer. Yet, so many people don't even make the connection as to how healthy eating habits affect our mood, and ultimately, our happiness. Really, I think sometimes people just choose to ignore it. I know I have.

I would say the majority of people know more about what they put in their car than what they put in their body. In fact, the poet John Kendrick Bangs was clever enough to write a poem on the subject way back in 1920. Ol' JKB backs my point up perfectly with these verses.

> You know the model of your car
> You know just what its powers are.
> You treat it with a deal of care
> Nor tax it more than it will bear.
> But as to self- That's different.
> Your mechanism may be bent,
> Your carbureter gone to grass,
> Your engine just a rusty mass.
> Your wheels may wobble and your cogs
> Be handed over to the dogs,
> And on you skip, and skid and slide,
> Without a thought of things inside.
> What fools indeed we mortals are
> To lavish care upon a car
> With ne'er a bit of time to see

About our own machinery!

So in summary, if you are an average, everyday teenager, here are a list of things that you know more about than the food you pile on your plate… or in your to-go paper bag:

- Twitter, Tweeting and the ever interesting, Retweet

- The Kardashians

- Whoever is into whoever at (fill in the blank) Jr. High

- Whoever is into whoever at (fill in the blank) High School

- Memes and Emojis

- Whatever the words B2K, Bae, TBH and LMS actually mean

- Your car, your friends' car, your parents' car, your toy car

- Your shoes and your friends' shoes and your

favorite NBA players' shoes

But I digress. All I'm saying is none of the things above really affect your long term happiness (and I love my basketball shoes as much as the next guy), but the eating habits you are creating now, absolutely will affect your long term happiness.

BALANCE

I once heard a story of a doctor who told his patient he needed to slow down and find balance in his life to reduce the stress of work. He suggested something like an hour of exercise a day and an hour of reading or some sort of wind down activity. The patient said, "Doctor, I don't have the time to relax! I have work to do!" The doctor, not missing a beat, responded, "Well, maybe you'll make the time when you're in a hospital bed."

That story really put everything into perspective for me. We can learn to rest now or one day our body will force us to rest. And I can guarantee your body won't take your busy schedule into consideration!

Balance is not something we find one day, it is something we create. If we wait on it, it will never happen. Balance is about choices, it's about setting priorities. Your actions reflect your priorities and what you really want out of life. If you say you REALLY want something, your actions better reflect it!

I know a woman who once said to me, "I will literally do ANYTHING to be happy!" I gave some suggestions that revolved around finding balance in her life, meaning a few life changes that were the cause of her stress. As soon as I finished, she blurted out, "I will literally do anything.... EXCEPT for that!" She may have said it out loud, but we all say things like that subconsciously, every single day! "I am completely willing to change, as long as it's not too inconvenient!"

Changing our priorities is a sign we are ready to change our lives. Prioritizing to create balance in your life is the simple act of deciding what has to be done in the way of necessary tasks in life and what is MOST important to your long term happiness. It all comes down to what truly matters.

First, you need to decide where you want to hit your home runs in life. What does that even mean? I have a dear friend who got his PhD from one of the most prestigious universities in the world. He told me that there were days in his first year where he would be so busy, he would schedule five minutes a day to think freely for himself. In despair, he turned to a close family member and got advice that changed his life. That same advice eventually changed my life and has, without a doubt, changed countless lives. "You have to decide where you want to hit home runs in life. Everything else needs to be a base hit! Your family, that's a home run that matters. Nothing you can do will replace the time with those you love. Your research? It's important, you should work hard on it, but someone will probably improve upon it, disprove it, or overshadow it within the next ten years. That's a home run that doesn't need to be hit!" Your health and happiness? Hit a home run! Binging ten episodes of the latest episode of whatever it is you are watching lately…. Probably shouldn't be a priority. In the case of my friend, he had to decide what he wanted to be remembered for in his life. In this case, he decided he wanted to be remembered for the relationships he's cultivated and the service he rendered to his fellow man. Once that priority was set, an amazing thing happened. Everything else in his life fell into place, including his friendships, health, school, work AND his research. Life is a marathon, so again, it's about deciding what's most important to YOU in the long run.

Time is the only commodity of which all people on the earth are given an equal amount, every single day- no strings attached. You are gifted 24 hours, 1440 minutes, 86,400 seconds (and just in case you're into this kind of thing, 8.64e+13 nanoseconds) 7 times a week, 365 days a year... You get the point.

However, what we decide to do with that time is what really defines us. It shows how committed we are to a happy life and not just a busy life. We may have the same amount of moments FOR happiness, but we don't equally have the same amount of happiness IN our moments. That decision is up to each of us.

SELF-REFLECTION: _____

_____

_____

_____

_____

_____

_____

_____

_____

_____

_____

_____

_____

_____

_____

_____

_____

_____

_____

_____

_____

_____

_____

_____

FOUNDATIONS OF THE HEART

"Service which is rendered without joy helps neither the servant nor the served. But all other pleasures and possessions pale into nothingness before service which is rendered in a spirit of joy."
- Mahatma Gandhi
Nonviolence Advocate and Leader of the Indian Independence Movement

The wonderful thing about the heart, the emotional side of our lives, is that there is an infinite capacity for our love to grow and multiply. Too often when times get tough, we turn inward and start asking, "Why me?" And we're not even talking about catastrophic events, we're talking about everyday things that we're not even going to remember in a week! Ever wake up five minutes late anyone?

It's a habit we create over time! We start asking, "Why me?", after the smallest setbacks, like stopping at a red light, or missing a question on a test, or, (GASP), getting a small stain on our shirt that no one but us will ever notice. We can easily choose to focus on the one thing that didn't go well instead of the 99 things that did. How much happier would we be if we simply reversed our focus?

For example, what if instead of asking, "Why did this happen to me?", we ask, "Why did this happen for me?" Maybe stopping at the red light kept you out of an accident, maybe missing a question on the test led you to a study group and a new friend, maybe getting a stain on our shirt made some freshman feel a little less awkward about the stain on his own shirt and you had no idea. In the meantime, maybe the stain gave you a good laugh because you realized that it was more funny than it was upsetting. You never know.

The happiest people in the world are those that choose to give freely to others, out of love, with no expectation of recognition. This is the case even when, or especially when, things aren't going their way. That is the definition of fueling the heart. In the words of the great John Wooden, "You can't live a perfect day until you do something for someone who will never be able to repay you." It's losing sight of yourself, and gaining insight and compassion into the lives of others that brings happiness.

Essentially, these are the people that in their life's trials could easily say, "Why me?", but instead, when making the decision on whether or not to begin sulking in despair, they think of all the good they can do in the world, and say, "Why not?"

Why not go out and try and make my friends smile? It will make them happy, and it will make me happy to brighten their day. Why not go out and perform a random act of kindness? The person to whom I give may never know it was me who lifted her burden, but her burden will be lifted. Isn't that what really matters?

Why not focus on what I CAN control and let go of what I can't? I bet I will find more satisfaction and peace when I am working hard at the things I CAN control.

Why not go out and watch a movie that will make me laugh? Laughing is a lot more fun (and healthy) than being upset.

There are two types of people in this world. The ones that wait for someone to come around to make them happy and the ones that go out and do their best to make other people's lives happier. Which one do you want to be? It doesn't take any special skill, just a desire. That ball is entirely, completely, 100 percent, without exception, in YOUR court!

GRATITUDE

One of the most proven and lasting ways people find happiness in their lives is by cultivating an attitude of gratitude! The incredible part of the positive effects of gratitude is that they apply equally to everyone. Each continent (though I don't know much about Antarctica's cultural history!) is filled with stories, poems, proverbs and lessons portraying the positive effects and universal need for gratitude.

Here are some examples:

"Gratitude is the heart's memory."

– French Proverb

"Forget injuries, never forget kindness."

– Chinese Proverb

"When eating fruit, think of the person who planted the tree."

– Vietnamese Proverb

"If you see no reason for giving thanks, the fault lies in yourself."

– Native American Proverb

"One can pay back the loan of gold, but one dies forever in debt to those who are kind."

– Malayan Proverb

"I complained I had no shoes until I met a man who had no feet."

– Persian Proverb

"Give thanks for a little and you will find a lot."

– Nigerian Proverb

And finally, whether it's a proverb or a bumper sticker, a shout out to all the educators out there….

"If you can read this, thank a teacher!"

– American Proverb/ Literal Truth/ Political
Poster/ A Thing That Teachers Say

Expressing gratitude, every day, even for the little things in life, creates a wonderful foundation of happiness on which you can build your life. This should be done with words AND with actions. President John F. Kennedy, 35th president of the United States, observed, "As we express our gratitude, we must never forget that the highest appreciation is not to utter words, but to live by them." Words of gratitude backed by action and actions of gratitude backed by words unite to transform our lives and our outlook of the world around us.

In an April 2015 article in Psychology Today by Amy Morin, LCSW, several of the scientifically proven benefits of an attitude of gratitude are simply laid out for us.

1. Grateful people have more opportunities for new and, often, lasting relationships.

2. Gratitude improves physical health.

FOUNDATIONS OF TEENAGE HAPPINESS

3. Gratitude improves mental health.

4. Gratitude increases your empathy and how much you care for other people, all while reducing anger and aggression.

5. Gratitude helps you sleep better.

6. Gratitude improves self-esteem.

7. Grateful people have reduced stress, and a higher sense of resilience to life's trials.

That's the end of Amy's list. So if I am reading the following breakdown right, and I'm pretty sure I am because I typed it out, I can make some powerful observations.

If you can develop a foundation in your life where gratitude is central to who you are, you will:

Create loving and lasting relationships, while increasing your empathy for others all while decreasing your stress, feelings of anger and jealousy. You will also improve your self-esteem, sleep better and become a healthier person across the board.

I don't know about you, but I think that describes

a person with incredible reason to be happy! And you can be that person! It's about setting the foundation, creating the habits and looking for opportunities to both be grateful and express that gratitude every day.

So let's talk about some everyday, practical ways that you can show gratitude and claim the incalculable benefits of living a grateful life. Here are ten to get you started! Feel free to add your own!

1. Write thank you notes expressing gratitude.

2. Express thanks for the little things in your life

3. Keep a gratitude journal. Write in it every night, including at least three things you are grateful for that day.

4. Recognize the people who make an immense impact on your life and let them know

5. Think about those from your past that have shaped you into who you are today and let them know.

6. Send three texts a day giving thanks for someone else's kindness.

7. Thank the unnoticed people around you.

8. Don't complain for 24 hours

9. Leave a little extra in your tip or a note thanking your server for the great job he did.

10. Give back to your elementary school with your time, showing how grateful you are for all the school and its staff did for you.

It's hard to go wrong when showing gratitude. The most important thing is that it's from the heart and given with sincerity. Happiness naturally follows the grateful soul. Do it daily and your life will be transformed! Make it a habit and your life will ALWAYS have meaning!

SERVICE

Many people have spent their entire lives looking for true happiness- the kind that endures forever. Gandhi knew this and taught a powerful lesson on the matter. "The best way to find yourself is to lose yourself in the service of others." True service, with no expectation of reward or recognition, but simply for the well-being of your fellow man, is one of the truest and noblest paths to authentic happiness.

Service comes down to a mentality you create. If cultivated it becomes a way of life. At that point, you very well might find yourself asking the questions Van Gough posed centuries ago. "How can I be useful, of what service can I be? There is something inside me, what can it be?"

Service transforms our vision and the currency by which we measure our lives. The renowned scientist, George Washington Carver understood the true way to measure one's success in life and by that same scale, to measure one's happiness. "It is not the style of clothes one wears, neither the kind of automobile one drives, nor the amount of money one has in the bank, that counts. These mean nothing. It is simply service that measures success." What if our main source of gratification wasn't measured by whether or not we have the newest phone, name brand clothes, or the most followers on Instagram, but instead by the number of people we've helped and whose days we've brightened? How would your life be different?

Another truth to live by: If we measure our lives in terms of people we've helped as opposed to materials we've collected, our life will be transformed. How do you think your life would be transformed with this kind of outlook? What's stopping you from trying?

Performing acts of kindness releases chemicals that cause you to feel happy and want to perform more kind acts. It's like a domino effect. Once you put in the effort to push down the first domino, the rest fall in natural course. Working up the desire to serve is the first step. Seeing people as more than just objects but as human beings. Seeing your fellow man, complete with the same desires, fears and ambitions that you have, is a close second step you need to take on this life altering journey.

When serving, you feel a sense of belonging, feel more empowered to a higher purpose. True service, with no thought of reward, helps you find inner peace in a world of pessimism and uncertainty. Service is contagious. When it spreads, lives are altered, souls are lifted, and light disperses darkness.

I have always been inspired by the pass-it-on principle. There was a time in my life when I was a young man and I needed a suit. I had no suit and no money for a suit, even from the second hand store. I received a call from a man I knew well, who told me to meet him at a certain clothing store in thirty minutes. I didn't know what the meeting was about, and we had never had this kind of meeting before, but I went. He walked me into the men's clothing section and said, pick a suit. I was shocked, I didn't even know he was aware of my predicament. I found a modest suit, he grabbed it from me and paid for it before I could even catch up with him. When I asked him if I could repay him, he told me, "My dear friend, someone did this for me many years ago when I was your age. And now I have the opportunity to do it for you. I don't want anything in return. The only thing I ask is that when you get the chance, you pass the kind act on to someone else." As I have tried to continue this legacy, sometimes I close my eyes and try to imagine the blue peaceful waters of a large and beautiful lake. The single drop of a pebble starts the ripple, I like to imagine it never ending. That wonderful man's contribution to me in my time of need dropped a pebble in the water, I don't plan on the ripple effects ever stopping.

Jeni Santi wrote an insightful piece in the October 2015 issue of Time Magazine on the subject of service and its link to authentic happiness. "There is a Chinese saying that goes: "If you want happiness for an hour, take a nap. If you want happiness for a day, go fishing. If you want happiness for a year, inherit a fortune. If you want happiness for a lifetime, help somebody."

For centuries, the greatest thinkers have suggested the same thing: Happiness is found in helping others.

"For it is in giving that we receive"

- Saint Francis of Assisi

"The sole meaning of life is to serve humanity"

- Leo Tolstoy

"We make a living by what we get; we make a life by what we give"

- Winston Churchill

"Making money is a happiness; making other people happy is a super happiness"

- Nobel Peace Prize recipient Muhammad Yunus

"Giving back is as good for you as for those you are helping, because giving gives you purpose. When you have a purpose- driven life, you're a happier person"

- Goldie Hawn

And so we learn early: It is better to give than to receive...But is there a deeper truth behind the truism?

The resounding answer is yes. Scientific research provides compelling data to support the anecdotal evidence that giving is a powerful pathway to personal growth and lasting happiness... Experiments show evidence that altruism is hardwired in the brain— and it's pleasurable. Helping others may just be the secret to living a life that is not only happier but also healthier, wealthier, more productive, and meaningful." That's the end of the Time article, in case you're curious! Now it's back to me my friends.

That is some incredible insight we ought to take seriously. And if you're curious (don't pretend like you're not!), altruism means the practice of selfless concern for the well-being of others. There's a reason we love superheroes, and again don't pretend like you don't! What do characters like Captain America, Batman, Superman, and Wonder Woman all have in common? Well, they are the clear career options of choice for just about every 10 year old in the world. But more importantly, they each have altruistic motivations. Or in other words, they aren't so concerned about themselves as much as they are concerned about using their skills and powers for the well-being of other people. Something inside you tells you that's the right way to live. Don't ignore that voice. There's a reason for it.

But do we need to be a superhero to change someone's life or to feel the happiness that flows from service? Well… no, absolutely not! And… umm…. Yes, for sure! Let me explain.

No, you don't need any superpowers to make a

difference in someone's life. And then a resounding Yes, because I can't think of anything more heroic than dedicating your time and your gifts to the well-being of others! Someone who gives selflessly, without any thought of reward, is the true definition of a superhero. Mother Theresa was one of those superheroes without a cape or a suit, but she was a hero in every sense of the word, touching and inspiring millions of lives until the day she died. Here is one thing this real life super hero said that has always touched my heart. "Spread love everywhere you go. Let no one ever come up to you without leaving happier." I challenge you to find someone more heroic.

It's daunting to think of changing millions of lives through our service. We can't let that stop us. Sometimes I like to think of service this way. No matter how big or small, if I can touch 5 lives a day then every week I am making 35 people's lives a little better. Over the course of a month, I can help 155 people, even if I am a stranger to them! Over the course of the year, someone committed to the 5 acts of service challenge will have affected 1825 lives for good. Add that up over a lifetime and it's impossible to ever think of your life's work as meaningless.

You don't have to commit to 5 acts a day (though it's really not a bad idea), but I invite you to commit to something, some number, some selfless gesture, something outside of yourself. In the inspired words of Nobel Prize winner, Wole Soyinka, "Human life has meaning only to that degree and as long as it is lived in the service of humanity." Don't suppress those thoughts you have to do good to others, to give, to serve. It is acting on those thoughts in the service of others that life's meaning is found and happiness is unlocked. A man you may have heard of, they call him William Shakespeare, said this, "How far that little candle throws his beams! So shines a good deed in a weary world!"

Giving it some thought and consideration, what are some ways that you can increase your service for others on a daily basis? You will, undoubtedly, come up with inspired and life changing ideas of your own. However, here are a few ideas to get you started. Just remember the most important rule, (seriously, get a highlighter or something) though service brings true and authentic happiness, it must never become about you. Ok, with that highlighted, underlined and starred, here are a few ideas to which you can add. You'll see principles of service in these stories, but I know you will also find other principles we've talked about as you look closely.

- **Give Anonymously** I am often asked to speak at high school awards ceremonies. I am always touched when an unknowing student receives a scholarship he didn't apply for from a family, organization or person that wishes to remain anonymous. How amazing is that? Year after year they are making a difference in the life of a high school senior and no one even knows who to thank. The simple thought that their scholarship can make a difference in someone's life makes them happy and is reward enough for their service. That's pretty amazing. You don't have to create a

FOUNDATIONS OF TEENAGE HAPPINESS

scholarship, but who says you can't? In either case, you understand the principle. We give because we want to serve, not because we want people to praise us for what we did.

- **Help When You See a Need** I was once with my younger brother in eastern Idaho where he was attending college. Here's something you need to know about eastern Idaho. It is abnormally, ridiculously, uncontrollably cold. It was April and there was a snow storm in full effect. I was sitting at the kitchen table as he and his best friend, who we grew up with, were looking out the window at all the cars getting stuck in the snow. Without saying a word to each other, they both began to put on their winter gear, boots and all, grab some chains and head out the door. Not wanting to be left behind and feeling there was work to be done, I did the same. With an old four wheel drive pickup truck, we spent the entire day pulling the cars of helpless strangers out of the snow, for free, one after another, hours on end. It was never spoken, but it was clear to all of us, the lesson we learn time and time again in life; when the right thing to do presents itself, you do it. Pushing cars on slippery ice while falling half the time, shoveling snow, hooking chains to hitches, helping direct traffic. I froze that day in the unforgiving winds of a blizzard. But I don't know if I have ever been happier.

- **Listen** Sometimes the greatest service we can give is to simply listen. Bryan H. McGill one of the most influential men in social media shares his thoughts on listening. "Too often we underestimate the power of a touch, a smile, a kind word, a listening ear, an honest compliment, or the smallest act of caring, all of which have the potential to turn a life around. Most people do not listen with the intent to understand; they listen with the intent to reply." I echo his sentiment and reiterate the last line of the quote. We listen to others because what they have to say is important. True service is listening to understand the human being in front of you, to really know him; her wants, desires, dreams, pains, heartache. When you listen halfheartedly, thinking about your reply instead of what's being said to you, you miss the opportunity to serve. Deep down everyone just wants to be understood. Being understood opens even a broken heart to a sense of happiness.

- **Befriend Others** I remember my family moving towards the end of the third grade. My mother was nice enough to drive the forty minutes each way so I could finish the school year with my class (Almost three hours a day in the car). But I knew that wouldn't last forever and that come the fall I would be in a whole new school, in a whole new community with kids I had never met. I was terrified and as the summer progressed, my fear only got worse. The first day of school, I walked into my class scared and alone. The wonderful teacher had left note cards with our names on our assigned desks. Grouped in fours, I sat down directly across from a young girl who had arrived at class just before me. She immediately reached out her hand and said, "I'm Samantha, it's really nice to meet you. What's your name?" Just like that I had a friend. All of my fear disappeared. I am still in debt to her this day for her service. She took a day that could have been miserable and turned it into a happy one just with her small gesture of friendship.

- **Give of Your Time** There are a million ways you can use your time. Here are just a few; video games, Netflix, staring at the wall, painting the wall, throwing a ball at the wall and letting it bounce back. Aside from the staring, they all sound pretty interesting despite the fact my gaming skills are severely limited to the oldest Super Mario Brothers on the original Nintendo. But, there are other things we can do with our time that bring so much more satisfaction. I'll give you one example from my life. When I was a junior in high school, I spent countless hours with one of my best friends at his house where his dad had his office as the town veterinarian. One day, probably after seeing us just sitting there throwing a ball against a wall, he said, "Boys, I have something for you to do." The ball stopped bouncing. We imagined cleaning out the large field on their property, unclogging irrigation ditches, walking dogs that had more bite than bark, but it wasn't any of that. He continued, "There is a client of mine who is a widow. She is very old, and I know she is having a tough time. I want the two of you to go down there, find out what she needs and take care of it." Us? A couple of 17 year old high school kids? What were we supposed to do? But he gave us the address, and we obediently went, not knowing what to expect. The house was old and in shambles. We knocked on the door, and five minutes later an elderly woman peeked through a small window. She reluctantly opened the door after we explained to her no less than five times who we were. Her house was disastrous, overrun by dust and grime. She invited us to sit down, we did, and visited with her for an hour, just listening to her stories, some from times gone by, some sad and depressing. We told her we wanted to help her. She told us she didn't have any money. We said we were going to do it for free and she, for the life of her, couldn't understand why. I don't know if we understood why. She cried and insisted we call her "Grandma" even though we had barely met her. Well, we went back, week after week. In her old age she would sometimes forget who we were, and we would have to start the process over again, but that was ok, we could see her becoming happier and happier every time we visited. We cleaned her house, pulled weeds, taught her how to use her TV, we fixed her air conditioning after recruiting a ringer that could do that kind of thing. We washed everything you can think of in a house, painted things, fixed meals, you name it. Sometimes, we just listened and we learned. Our dear, adopted Grandma eventually passed away, but we were her "boys," sometimes she called us her angels, and we never left without receiving a frail but tender hug on the way out the door. I don't think my friend and I understood the opportunity we had been given, how happy it made us, how happy it made her. I'm positive his Dad knew and had a sense of the impact it would have on the rest of our lives. Needless to say, we are both forever grateful we got to spend those countless hours serving our dear "Grandma" instead of throwing a ball against a shed, talking about how boring life happened to be.

- **Stand Up For a Good Cause** There is a university I'm acquainted with that, to me, epitomizes standing up for a good cause. I think its actions could easily be replicated at a number of high schools across the country. This particular university is known for its innovation. It also happens to be located in what many would call a rougher part of town. The opportunity presented itself as the university grew, to relocate its campus or at least expand its campus into a much richer, nicer part of the city. They chose not to. Instead they stood up for a good cause, saying, in essence, this is where our campus has always been, we are a part of this community and as part of this community we will do our part to rejuvenate our neighborhood and give back in any way we can. Not only has the administration been true to its word but so has the undergraduate population, many of which are teenagers like you. Students are volunteering in the local elementary schools. They are building houses, helping the elderly, giving time at community centers, and painting over graffiti in between tutoring at risk students. By the way, this university is noted for having one of the highest overall student happiness ratings in the country. Not a coincidence. At the high schools in the community, students are moving from "at risk" to receiving full ride scholarships to the university in their own back yard. Jobs are being given to the local population, allowing families to spend more time together, not having to drive miles and miles to find work. The school is investing in alumni who start businesses in their neighborhood, and the employment rate is rising amongst members of the neighborhood because of those businesses. You don't have to replicate everything this university is doing, but as they say, the main thing is to keep the main thing the main thing. In this case, the main thing is when it comes to standing up for what's right, you will always be happier in the long run doing SOMETHING, even when it seems inconvenient or even justified to do nothing.

- **Give to Youth** I once had the opportunity to work with an incredible third grade student with special needs. He was a nonverbal little guy with a heart of gold and a spirit of freedom that often found him running out the classroom door at exactly all the wrong times. I was brought in to work with him. Though I was assigned a certain number of hours, I found myself staying after because this young fellow's happy spirit was infectious. I worked tirelessly, making up little chants and using little phrases, to try and help him to form words. The consensus amongst the experts in his life was that he COULD talk, he just didn't want to. His teachers and aides were at a loss for what to do. This had gone on for nearly four years. After a few days, it occurred to me that deep down, I felt I could connect with him in a meaningful way. In return, he would light up and put his hands in the air, screaming with excitement every time I walked through the door, and he would get up out of his seat and run, full speed, to give me a big hug. So I guess, we were off to a good start. It made my day, literally, every time; it filled my life with joy. One day, after weeks of working with my young friend, I was sharing with him some rhymes I thought he would like. Out of nowhere, and to the shock of the seven aides in the room, he began to repeat back to me, shouting the rhymes, complete with the hand motions I had no idea he had even picked up on! He continued and continued and continued, increasing with enthusiasm after every turn. I was smiling from ear-to-ear and in tears, I looked around the room and the whole class had stopped to watch this miracle take place. There wasn't a dry eye in the room. He talked that day for twenty minutes straight. When his dear mother came to pick him up, she cried when his aide told her the story saying she had been waiting for that day for what felt like forever. When I saw her the next day, she again had tears in her eyes. She told me they had gone out for a walk and instead of dragging his feet like he normally did, he was running to the top of the little hills jumping up and down yelling the positive expressions I had taught him. She hugged me and thanked me. It was probably the most sincere thank you I have received in my life, and it still fills my heart with overwhelming happiness every time I think about it. But, let me make something clear, though this experience may seem miraculous, there are countless opportunities out there for you to have similar experiences. I don't know if something similar would have happened if I was with another student, I don't know if this student would have responded to another adult. All I do know is, nothing would have happened if I hadn't taken the opportunity. Kids need someone to believe in them. Why not you? Go out and show the elementary school kids, younger than you, how much you believe in them. Read to them, play with them, listen to them. You will become their heroes! Give of your time to the youth that will inevitably look up to you as a role model. Don't do it in passing, but with the desire to REALLY be there for them, and watch how the light of happiness overcomes you and changes your life. It did for me.

- **Champion the Unnoticed** This story came from a high school reunion I attended. I wasn't even aware of the events that took place way back in high school! I think it's a testament to the friends I surrounded myself with and their inclusive nature. So here's what happened; a friend of mine came up to me and some close friends at the reunion and said, "You know, you guys changed my life." This man was one of the best I knew, so I said,

"You changed my life, my friend." That was true for a variety of reasons, but he dismissed it. He said, "No I'm serious. When I moved to town, I didn't know a single person, and I came from a school that only had a couple of hundred kids, and I knew everyone. I spent the first few months hanging out with the only people I could find, and they were horrible influences. Most days, I ate lunch by myself. Then one day, one of you guys came up to me after class and just started a conversation with me. That changed everything. You invited me to hang out, and the entire course of my high school career was changed. I went from being the most miserable I had ever been in my life to the most happy. I don't want to think about what would have happened if we didn't all become friends." That shook me to the core. First, he spent months basically alone before any of us noticed him. Second, I knew him in class but had no idea what he was going through. I can honestly say this kid was one of those kids that made me a happier person because of his genuine nature and goodness. Yet he went unnoticed. I can't remember who started the conversation or what class he was talking about, but I can't imagine going through high school without him. The point is, I missed an opportunity. You don't have to. I guarantee there are dozens of kids on your campus that feel unnoticed, maybe even invisible. No one should feel that way. If you feel that way and you want to be happier, go reach out to someone else who's in the same situation. If you don't feel invisible but you want to be happier while making someone else happy, go find the unnoticed and make sure they know they are not only noticed but included with you and your friends. A philosophy to live by: There's always another seat at the table.

- **Give to the Elderly**   I once had the opportunity to visit with a group of teenagers who, to me, seemed different than other teenagers I had worked with. Every weekend, they went to the senior citizens center. One day, I decided to accompany them just to see what was going on. We went into the big recreation room, and I sat back and watched as one of the teenagers served as DJ. What took place was one of the liveliest dances I have ever seen. The teenagers went around the room dancing with the residents, and the residents began to dance with each other. It was amazing! Stories were swapped, songs were sung, and time seemed to roll back. I am not much of a dancer myself, but a nice older lady in a wheel chair asked me to accompany her in one of her favorite songs from the swing era. How could I resist? I was caught up in the moment, dancing the night away- well until about seven when people started to head to bed- and heard stories of what it was like to grow up in the great depression, serve in WWII, attend school in a one-room school house, raise children, and then become great-grandparents. I had the time of my life! It became overwhelmingly clear that these teenagers were infinitely cooler than me. I asked the young lady that seemed to be the head of the group, why do you all continue to do this every week? I mean, why be here when there are so many other things you could be doing? She answered without missing a beat, "Didn't you see the look on their faces when we walked in? Didn't you see the looks on our faces when we left? It makes them happy and it makes us happy." It really was that simple.

The words of Swami Vivekananda encompass the entire essence of how service contributes to our happiness and success. "The great secret of true success, of true happiness, is this: the man or woman who asks for no return, the perfectly unselfish person, is the most successful." And I would add, the most happy…

SELF-REFLECTION: _____

FOUNDATIONS OF THE SOUL

*"What lies behind us and what lies ahead of us are tiny matters
compared to what lives within us."*
- Henry David Thoreau
The Great American Poet

The soul, in simplicity, is the center of who we are as human beings. It is that part of our existence that makes us unique, an individual of grand potential and worth amongst the billions of stars in the universe, and fellow passengers on the earth. Happiness finds its natural home in the light of the open hearted soul. It is the energy that makes up our passions. When we feed it, that passion manifests itself in a beautiful life full of energy and purpose. Your soul becomes a conduit for peace, and happiness follows abundantly. Within your soul lie your virtues, your morals, and your beliefs about life and humanity. It is our spiritual side, it can't always be explained, but it can be felt, daily, even constantly, if we are listening.

In the classic words of the famed Irish playwright, Oscar Wilde, "Ordinary riches can be stolen; real riches cannot. In your soul are infinitely precious things that cannot be taken from you." The only way to lose your soul, so to speak, is if you give it away by choosing to go against what your very being is telling you is right.

I, personally, am no believer in moral relativism. In other words, I really think there is a right and a wrong, especially when it comes to how we treat others. I have a feeling you know it too! I heard a story once that helped me understand the idea a little better, as we are all given the choice to do what we know is right or to do the easily rationalized thing that we deep down know is wrong. The story goes like this, a man told his friend, I feel like there are two wolves fighting inside of me, one representing right and the other wrong. His friend asked, which one wins? The man answered simply but firmly, The One I Feed.

It's no different for you and for me. Without being too cliché, while also being really cliché, we have to follow our heart. How else can we expect to find inner peace? How else are we to truly expect happiness? Sometimes doing the right thing comes at a time when we are literally all alone. We have all had the opportunity to do something we know is wrong, and the thought often comes into our mind, what's the harm? No one will ever know! What we do after that thought defines us. Oprah said it best, in a way that only she can, "Real integrity is doing the right thing, knowing that nobody's going to know whether you did it or not." In those moments, you know your soul is on a path to or dwelling safely in the rich and abundant forest of authentic happiness.

To reiterate the point, standout college quarterback turned member of the House of Representatives, J.C Watts, shared some profound guidance, "Character is doing the right thing when nobody's looking. There are too many people who think that the only thing that's right is to get by, and the only thing that's wrong is to get caught!" In those moments when you do the right thing without a single person in sight, you know people can trust you and more importantly, that you can trust yourself. Happiness is the natural consequence of true integrity.

I want you to be happy, and I believe you can start being happier right now, or else I obviously wouldn't have written this book. I believe that cultivating happiness through the soul, just as you do through the heart and the body and the mind, is crucial to that worthy endeavor. The four work together in perfect unison, they are so much stronger combined than they are isolated.

So how do we find happiness through our soul? The answer is, I don't think we find it (EVEN BIGGER GASP!). Someone once said, "The foolish man looks for happiness out in the distance, the wise man grows it under his feet." So if we want to find happiness in the depths of our soul, we need to grow it. In order to grow that kind of happiness, we need to feed our souls, just like anything else we want to grow.

I once walked through the National Redwood Forest. Giant. Breathtaking. Majestic. Gorgeous. All words that could be used to describe the experience. A thought occurred to me that the entire forest probably came from one seed. Think about it! One seed, given proper soil, life giving water and abundant light can grow to become a mighty redwood and then produce other redwoods. In theory, millions upon millions of redwoods whose root systems interlock to create support for the entire forest and a powerful experience for anyone blessed to behold its awe inspiring presence.

Your life can be like those incredible redwoods. Tall and confident, happy in its existence, united in its surroundings. You just need to consistently and purposefully feed your soul. Well, how do we feed our souls? There are plenty of things you can do to nourish your soul, just the way a tree is nourished in its growth. Some are unique to you personally, so please feel encouraged to add to this list, write in the margins, glue in pages, overall, make it personal to you! With that said, here are some foundations I think are important for anyone looking to grow happiness in her soul.

AUTHENTIC RELATIONSHIPS

You are bombarded with social media almost

every minute of every day. You can stream your favorite TV shows on demand. You probably text far more than you ever talk on the phone. Headphones are in your ears constantly. You tweet, post status updates (#readingthisbook, #changingmylife), share videos, and probably do a bunch of other stuff people over 30 don't even get; but, how well are you really connecting with your friends?

We can become so disconnected from the rest of the world that we can lose sight of the fact that we aren't the only ones in it!

You might rightly ask, what is an authentic relationship? Great question, I'll answer it for you. An authentic relationship goes far beyond the superficial. It's a relationship that's real, genuine, and heart-to-heart. An authentic relationship is two-sided, with people mutually caring for one another on a deep and lasting level. They are built off of wonderful experiences and also trials and tougher experiences. They are built on trust, respect, and loyalty. What they are not built on are "likes," shared life hacks, or occasional snapchats.

Here's a great saying: We can't make the mistake of confusing activity with productivity. That's good advice for work and school, but the same thing applies to our relationships. We can share everything we want to online, and social media is an incredible tool in building friendships when used correctly, but if we aren't really connecting with our friends and family, it's simply activity. That activity essentially amounts to nothing over time. It's important to aim for substance. The activity itself doesn't bring happiness, it only makes us feel like we're busy in search of happiness, while really we're just going through the motions. The substance, when we connect with people on a real one-on-one level, that's what creates the happiness we crave. That's what feeds the soul.

How do I cultivate authentic relationships? You ask with a stoic look in your eyes. Solid question. Here are some principles to live by.

BE A FRIEND FOR THE RIGHT REASONS

Treat your friends the way you KNOW you should. Like they are important to you. Like their time matters. Like their feelings matter. Like their future matters, and you plan to be a part of it! Don't be the person that reaches out only when they need something! Think of all the classic friendships; Burt and Ernie; Tom Sawyer and Huckleberry Finn; Cory, Topanga, and Shawn (google it, the show was amazing); Harry, Ron, and Hermione; Jazzy Jeff and the Fresh Prince; Tina Fey and Amy Poehler; Peanut butter and Jelly. What do they all have in common? It's obvious! Buzz and Woody's "You Got a Friend in Me" song, applies equally to every single one of them.

A mentor of mine told me something I'm never going to forget. He said, "You love people and you use money. You never, ever reverse the two." In other words, our life is in shambles the moment we start to love money and use people.

It doesn't have to be money. When we start loving someone's car and using him for it, we have lost our way. When we love someone's popularity and use it for our own entrance into the exclusive lunch table, we have lost our way. When we are constantly thinking of what others can do for us and forget that our happiness comes from helping others in their trials, we have lost our way.

On the exact opposite end, when we love our friends and use our combined talents to do good in the world, we find happiness. When we love our friends and use our personalities to build each other up, we find happiness. The distinction between the two ways of life makes all the difference. We're talking about some of the worst kind of misery and the best kind of joy.

Artist Kahlil Gibran made the same point decades ago, "Friendship is always a sweet responsibility, never an opportunity." Sometimes we are on the wrong end of a bad friendship. That's ok. Make new friends. The company you keep defines you. Start with a smile and build from there. I promise you there are people out there who will love you for who you are and not what you have or don't have. Don't give up, no, don't ever give up. Often those friends are just waiting for you to take the first step in approaching them.

One of my best friendships of all time started just like this at our freshman orientation of high school.

Me, "Hey man, do you want to stand together so we look like a group." Him, "Yeah, good idea." Thousands of hours of amazing times, deep conversations, road trips, and the best senior prank ever pulled in the history of the world followed that, now, historic moment. Come to think of it, someone should put a plaque on that exact spot!

HAVE CONFIDENCE IN WHO YOU ARE

Look, if you are into social media, then you are going to be tempted to compare your worst day with someone else's supposed perfect life on Insta. That is a recipe for disaster. Let me break it down for you. First, EVERYONE has bad days on occasion, and second, people only post the very best of the best of their life online. Nobody posts their C- from their chemistry test, or post the fact they can't even spell chemistrie. No one posts about bad hair days or pictures of themselves being angry or frustrated. The majority of people are literally posting random stuff to make you and everyone else think their life is perfect. Don't compare yourself to that fake life, and don't be the person that posts constantly about a fake life!

In the words of actress Hayley Hasselhoff, "It's all about confidence and how you feel about yourself. There's no such thing as a perfect woman. I like imperfections- that's what makes you unique." That's not something we see often in the world of social media, where you're the star and you get to put on a show portraying your life anyway you want. So here's the deal, if you can prove one of your friends literally has a perfect life with no down days, no rejection, no trials, no awkward moments; write me at theytotallyfooledyou@noone'slifeisperfect.org, we'll put their face on the first page of this book. But since that's not going to happen, knock it off! Stop comparing what you think are your worst moments to someone else's fake internet best moments!

The old doctor himself, Mr. Dr. Seuss said it best (Just real quick, do we even know if he was a real doctor? Or is it like a Pepper kind of doctor? Or did his parents name him Doctor trying to send him a message about their retirement? And if I were to name the son I don't have Super Genius, what message does that send? Actually, since my last name's Catt, that would make him Super Genius Catt, which sounds like a horrible movie I would never see, so let's just scratch that whole idea). I give him credit for these lines because, I mean, it's way more inspirational than Hop on Pop. "Today you are You, that is truer than true. There is no one alive who is Youer than You."

So have some confidence in who you are! Be proud of it! There is literally no one in the world who is the same as you. You have no reason to change yourself just to fit into someone else's idea of what you should be. Judy Garland understood this. She said, "Always be a first-rate version of yourself, instead of a second-rate version of somebody else." To try and become someone else is overrated! That's not an authentic relationship! In fact, that is denying the world of what you have to give. What only YOU can give.

Renowned psychologist and survivor of the Holocaust, Viktor E. Frankl, inspirationally taught this principle to live by. "Everyone has his own specific vocation or mission in life; everyone must carry out a concrete assignment that demands fulfillment.

Therein he cannot be replaced, nor can his life be repeated, thus, everyone's task is unique as his specific opportunity to implement it." Those opportunities that only you can fulfill, come every day, if you're looking for them. No one can replace you. I repeat, with more enthusiasm, no one can replace you!

It's natural to be insecure. It's normal for you to not know exactly what you want to do this weekend, much less your entire life! Don't worry about it! You can be confident in who you are right now. We're all a work in progress! When that fact clicks, and you have confidence anyway, you are ready to contribute to authentic relationships! And remember, authentic relationships are built and cultivated, the happiness follows abundantly!

So in the words of our old friend The Doctor (Seuss), "Kid you'll move mountains!" All you need is a little confidence in yourself!

ACCEPT PEOPLE FOR WHO THEY ARE

It's true, you are the only you, but here's something that will blow your mind... Everyone else is the only them! Another key to real, lasting, authentic relationships is to accept people for who they are and NOT what you want them to be. William Shakespeare understood it, "A friend is one that knows you as you are, understands where you have been, accepts what you have become, and still, gently allows you to grow."

In truth, we fail to accept people for who they are all the time. It's sad. But it's still true. The good news is, once we understand that we do it, we can change it! So let's try and understand it...

Do you ever find yourself thinking things like this?

- I wish (fill in the blank) would text me back quicker!

- If only (fill in the blank) would remember to do their chores!

- If only (fill in the blank) would come to more school activities!

- If only (fill in the blank) would feel the way I feel about (whatever social topic)!

- And here is my personal favorite I catch myself doing all the time; if only (said politician) would vote (fill in whatever ideology upon which the speech of my soapbox is based) then the world would be a better place!

In my example, what good does it do for me to talk at the TV and wish someone would do something differently when his entire life he has been on the opposite end of the spectrum from me? The answer for 100 points= It does no good. I need to accept the reality that he is who he is, and he is going to do what he does.

In other news, it's natural to want others to be a little more caring towards the things we care about, to push themselves a little bit harder when we feel they aren't reaching their full potential, or to be a little less hard on themselves when you see perfectly well that they are doing just fine. Sometimes it's appropriate to encourage people in a loving, empowering way. But, at the end of the day, it is entirely their choice to make, and not yours, as to whether or not they want to change. To ignore that truth, that people have the right to choose, will only lead to heartache, resentment, anger, and frustration, probably for both of you.

We don't have to agree with someone to accept her. We don't have to support her in her horrible behavior to accept her either. And we definitely should never put ourselves, our values, our health, or our families in harm's way in the name of acceptance. Sometimes, it just comes down to the fact, that it is what it is, you accept people for who they are then you go your way, and they'll go their way. That's still acceptance.

Again, the bottom line is we accept people for who they really are and not what we wish they would be. The good, the bad, and the ugly (also a great soundtrack; look it up on Youtube). You're probably still going to be sad, you are definitely going to wish things were different, you may even be angry, but in the end, you'll find peace, authenticity, and ultimately, inner happiness by viewing people for who they really are, what they really stand for, and for the decisions they are actually making. And you never know, sometimes just being there for someone can start him on the road to a better life, a happier life.

So why not try this? Think of whoever you want and say out loud or in your head or in writing or in painting if you can somehow make that work, "I accept you (fill in the blank) for who you are, the good, the bad, and everything in between. I don't know the road you've walked. I don't know every experience that has made you who you are. And, I don't need to agree with you on everything, and I get that, but nevertheless I accept you."

That is the foundation, and maybe, the true definition of an authentic relationship. The term, "keeping it 100;" I think this is what it's all about. But when you think about it, doesn't it feel liberating? Doesn't it make us a little happier to know we are seeing things as clear as we can?

WHAT REALLY MATTERS

Another crucial way we feed our souls is by constantly, even daily, putting things that matter most, first in our lives. We talked about hitting the right home runs earlier, so you can view these as the home runs in your life. They can be friends, family, good causes, our health, and countless other things, but you know better than me what those things are, so what good does it do me to try and tell you what should matter most? Instead, I'll tell you about the things in my life and the lives of others. You can see if they ring true to you.

Friends: You now know how to be an authentic friend. But let's just talk about how good friends affect our happiness. We all feel a need to belong, it is part of our nature. Good friends create bonds that lift our spirits and bring us belonging and happiness. We can be that friend to others. We don't need to be extroverts to make this happen; it has nothing to do with going to parties or dances and everything to do with being with people who just get us. Our friends can and should be a diverse group. The point is to be grateful for who we have in our lives. Novelist Marcel Proust said, "Let us be grateful to people who make us happy, they are the charming gardeners who make our souls blossom." A blossoming soul, is no doubt, a well-nourished, happy soul.

Doing the Right Thing: Our conscience will always be clear when we are standing up for what we know is the right thing to do. Sometimes, it's not what we do that contributes to our unhappiness, it's what we don't do. Read this poem by Margaret A. Sangster, called "The Sin of Omission" and see what you think.

It isn't the thing you do, dear;
It's the thing you leave undone,
Which gives you a bit of heartache
At the setting of the sun.
The tender word forgotten,
The letter you did not write,
The flower you might have sent, dear,
Are your haunting ghosts to-night.

The stone you might have lifted
Out of brother's way,
The bit of heartsome counsel
You were hurried too much to say;

The loving touch of the hand, dear,
The gentle and winsome tone,
That you had no time nor thought for,
With troubles enough of your own.

The little acts of kindness,
So easily out of mind;
Those chances to be angels
Which every one may find
They come in night and silence
Each chill, reproachful wraith
When hope is faint and flagging
And a blight has dropped on faith.

For life is all too short, dear,
And sorrow is all too great;
To suffer our great compassion
That tarries until too late;
And it's not the thing you do, dear,
It's the thing you leave undone,
Which gives you the bit of heartache
At the setting of the sun.

Now on the other hand, let's read this poem by Emily Dickenson, who shows us that even the smallest things bring happiness to the soul and meaning to life. Standing up for a good cause doesn't have to be a huge gesture, but it is absolutely essential. Again, read it and see what you think. It's called, "If I Can Stop One Heart from Breaking."

If I can stop one heart from breaking,
I shall not live in vain;
If I can ease one life the aching,
Or cool one pain,
Or help one fainting robin
Unto his nest again,
I shall not live in vain.

Stand up for what you know is right, keep your head high, put service first, live your truth. These are some of the things that matter most. You may not win them all, but you will never win if you never try (For example I am undefeated in baseball, I have never lost a game! I've also never played in an official baseball game, which makes it way less impressive). When you make it a priority to keep your integrity intact, you ARE going to be happy!

Family: Maybe your parents are amazing examples. Maybe they are horrible examples. Maybe you have tons of brothers and sisters. Maybe you are an only child. View family the way YOU need to view it. In my own life, I was raised quite a bit by my grandparents, my mother, a great-aunt in her late eighties, parents of friends, coaches, teachers. Somehow all of these people came to be a part of my family, and I consider myself to be the luckiest guy in the world. I had countless role models to look up to, and I got to pick and choose what to emulate.

I can say with absolute confidence that one of the things that has made me happiest in my life, is not taking these people for granted but cherishing them and acknowledging all they have given me and done for me. They have been my light in the darkness and the support when I begin to fall. Putting them first has been paramount in growing happiness under my feet.

Michael J. Fox didn't have to go back to the future to say with certainty, "Family is not an important thing. It's Everything."

FINDING PURPOSE

Finding purpose in our life is the last of the happiness ingredients I want to talk about when it comes to feeding our souls. Notice how I said, finding purpose, not finding A purpose. There's a difference. You're a teenager. You have time to define, refine, live and discover a purpose in life. Right now, just focus on finding purpose in the things you enjoy, in who you are, in what you give.

Someone once said, "Find yourself, and be that." That's great, but how do we find ourselves? Be true to what you love and who you are. We find our purpose through figuring out how we can leave a mark on the world through the gifts that WE bring. Purpose really comes down to helping other people and the world in general. I firmly believe that because I've seen it thousands of times.

As a teenager, you have time to find that purpose!

In fact, it's never too late to find your purpose. But you shouldn't feel rushed. Essentially, your job is to experience as much as you can. Try things! Decide what you like and what you don't like. You don't need to pick a career tomorrow, you just need to start the process of deciding what kinds of things you enjoy. Helping people? Building things? Traveling and learning about new cultures? Cooking? There are literally limitless possibilities. Happiness comes when you can answer the question, How can I use this thing I love to make a difference in the lives of other people?

Your head is going to tell you a lot of things, but your heart and soul are the key to determining purpose. Are you not sure what even interests you? That's ok! Here are some questions that might help you figure it out:

- What do you want to do when no one is telling you what to do? (Sleeping and eating don't count!)
- What kinds of things are you happiest doing?

- What makes you feel alive?
- What do you think about when your mind drifts off?
- If money and time didn't matter, what would you do?

WHEN HAVE YOU BEEN THE HAPPIEST IN YOUR LIFE?

I love what I do. But it took me a while to figure it out. I love speaking to teenagers. I love coaching basketball. I love passing on knowledge. What does that all boil down to? I love teaching. In any form, I'm all about it. But if I was teaching for no reason, I wouldn't be happy at all. So what am I missing that takes it to the next level? I love teaching to help people change their lives. I love seeing people progress. I love seeing them become happier. In my mind, that's purpose.

But if purpose is intrinsically about helping other people, there are millions of ways we can do that. People that get it, could potentially be saying things like this:

I love building schools because that is where the

future of America will start to live out their dreams, and I get to help them be a part of that.

I love cooking food because when people are eating my food they are happy and together.

I love painting because I know that what I'm doing not only brings me joy, but it brings joy to other people.

I love fixing cars because I know I am keeping families safe on the road and easing their stresses, that makes them happier and it makes me happy, too.

I love working in the library, no one may see what I do, but I know the books I am putting on the shelves are going to make people smile, think, learn, and change for the better. Could anything make me happier?

It's all in how we view the things we do, and especially, the things we like to do. The key is seeing how those things can make a difference in the lives of others. The Dali Lama (I had an amazing experience with him, ask me about it sometime) said it best, "The purpose of this life is to be happy." We achieve that happiness through serving others with purpose.

SELF-REFLECTION: _____

_____

_____

_____

_____

_____

_____

_____

_____

_____

_____

_____

_____

_____

_____

_____

_____

_____

_____

_____

_____

_____

SECTION 3
CONCLUSION

IT IS GOOD TO HAVE AN END TO JOURNEY TOWARD, BUT IT IS THE JOURNEY THAT MATTERS IN THE END.

- URSULA K. LE GUIN
WORLD RENOWNED AUTHOR

CONCLUSION

"All endings are also beginnings, we just don't know it at the time."
- Mitch Albom
Author of Tuesdays with Morrie

As you have learned, happiness is not a simple action, it is a way of life! We should never give up or ever get discouraged. Some days will be amazing, others won't. But that isn't the point. We can be overall happy people through all of it! Never give up, my young friends, never ever give up on the happy life you desire!

This poem by "The People's Poet," Edgar Guest, might provide some inspiration in challenging times. It is appropriately titled, "Don't Quit."

When things go wrong,
as they sometimes will,
When the road you're trudging

seems all uphill,

When funds are low and the debts are high,

And you want to smile but you have to sigh,

When care is pressing you down a bit,

Rest if you must, but don't you quit.

Life is queer with its twists and turns,

As every one of us sometimes learns,

And many a failure turns about,

When he might have won if he'd stuck it out.

Don't give up, though the pace seems slow -

You may succeed with another blow.

Often the goal is nearer than

It seems to a faint and faltering man;

Often the struggler has given up

When he might have captured

the victor's cup,

And he learned too late,

when the night slipped down,

How close he was to the golden crown.

Success is failure turned inside out -

The silver tint of the clouds of doubt,

And you never can tell how close you are -

It may be near when it seems afar;

So stick to the fight when you're hardest hit -

It's when things seem worst

that you mustn't quit.

YOUR NEXT STEPS

So, what are the steps you need to take right now, this very moment, to create a happy life? Here are two lines I want you to remember.

1. Nothing beats beginning like beginning.

2. Nothing changes if nothing changes.

You just need to start, somewhere, anywhere! Make a change; try one thing today, and another thing tomorrow. Why not? Life is an adventure! We are meant to have experiences that shape us and help us to become our best selves. Mary Kay Ash, a pioneering business women with incredible vision and an adventurous spirit said, "Most people live and die with their music still un-played. They never dare to try." This life is about trying, experiencing, and giving! As Henry Ford said, "Whether you think you can or you can't, you're probably right." So go for it. Make someone's day better. Write a thank you note. Be a friend to the friendless. Don't sit around and think of what you could do, just get up and do something! Play the music you were meant to play! Now that you have the foundations, it's time to close the book, set it on your desk, and get busy building a happy life!

ABOUT THE AUTHOR

Scott Catt is a cofounder and partner of the Allazo Group. Born and raised in Tucson, Arizona, Scott is a graduate of Brigham Young University and has done his masters work in Organizational Behavior at the University of London and Cambridge. Through the course of his studies, Scott has focused his attentions on happiness and leadership and has sought to bridge the gap between the styles and strategies of great leaders in the past and principle based application in the modern worlds of education and business. A passionate educator, Scott has led teachers and administrators in several educational institutions, and as a business professional, has served as a Senior

Vice President at national companies. He is fluent in Spanish and has diverse experience working with peoples and organizations from North and South America, Africa, and Europe. A prolific speaker, he has presented and trained at a wide variety of events and conferences, but his passion is speaking to teenagers! Before co-founding the Allazo Group, Scott worked for a top global training and development consulting firm.

43103690R00087

Made in the USA
Lexington, KY
24 June 2019